D0125099

Rose-Colored Glasses

Dell loves the birds, squirrels and other small creatures in the woods near her home. She returns a fallen baby bird to its nest, and rescues a bee whose wing is stuck on a thorn. At the brook she finds a rose-colored stone. When she looks through it she can see the fairy world and understand fairy words. Deeny Dew, the undine, makes the pretty stone into a pair of rose-colored glasses for Dell. When wearing them she seems the same size as the fairies and brownies. She also learns how the ants, bees and butterflies live. With Wimpy, her best friend, she sails away on a cloud boat to a castle where the patterns of music and everything on earth are made. She and Wimpy learn that all creatures of the woods and meadows are important in helping to make nature beautiful. Finally on his birthday Wimpy is given a pair of rose-colored glasses also, because he has been kind to every living thing.

Ruby L. Radford has written fifty books for children and young adults, as well as many short stories and serials. In 1969 she was voted "Author of the Year" by the Dixie Council of Authors and Journalists.

Books by Ruby L. Radford

THE ENCHANTED HILL (A Quest Book for Children)

JULIETTE LOW : GIRL SCOUT FOUNDER

THE SECRET OF PEACH ORCHARD PLANTATION

THE SECRET OF OCEAN HOUSE

and 45 other books for children and young adults

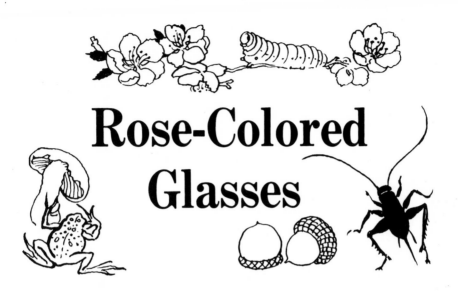

Rose-Colored Glasses

by
Ruby Lorraine Radford

illustrated by
Iris Weddell White

A QUEST Book for Children

Published under a grant from The Kern Foundation

THE THEOSOPHICAL PUBLISHING HOUSE
Wheaton, Ill., U.S.A.
Madras, India/London, England

© The Theosophical Publishing House 1970
All rights reserved
First edition 1939
Second revised edition 1970
The Theosophical Publishing House, Wheaton, Illinois,
is a department of
The Theosophical Society in America
Library of Congress Catalog Card Number: 79-110698
ISBN: 0-8356-0029-7
Manufactured in the United States of America

Dedicated to
All children who are kind
to every living thing

CONTENTS

Chapter 1

The Magic Stone

Dell ran out the garden gate. She looked down the path and into the woods. Where were her after-school playmates? She was sorry her best friend, Wimpy, could not run and play for a while. His leg had been broken in a car accident. Maybe the others were playing on the grapevine swing. When she ran on to the woods, no one was there.

They were not down the hill by the lily pool. Dell looked behind the bushes. They were not in the brush-arbor playhouse. Were they playing tricks on her? She thought she heard someone giggle.

This made Dell cross. She tossed back her golden hair. Her blue eyes flashed. She caught the grapevine swing and shook it angrily.

"Come down!" she called. "I know somebody's hiding from me."

Suddenly she heard a faint "Tweet! Tweet!"

Something tumbled through the leaves and fell at her feet. It was a wee bird. She had shaken it from its nest.

"Tweet! Tweet!" the baby bird kept crying.

His wings fluttered. But he could not fly back to his nest. Dell picked him up very gently. He was such a tiny, helpless little thing. She could feel his heart beating fast. Then a loud bird call came from the branches above. Wings brushed past Dell's cheek. The mother bird had seen her baby in Dell's hands.

How Dell wanted to keep it for her own! But the mother bird wanted her baby back. Dell tucked the helpless thing in the pocket of her shorts. She climbed the grapevine and scrambled up into the tree.

The mother bird pecked her on the back. She did not know Dell was trying to help. Two other birds stuck their open mouths out of the nest. Quickly Dell returned the third bird to his nest. The mother bird chirped her thanks while Dell climbed down.

Dell could hear a happy bird song as she skipped back to the lily pool. She felt happy now, too. She forgot she had been lonely. The woods were so full of wonderful things. The hawthorn bush had wee green buds on it. Sweetness of blossoms filled the air. A rabbit jumped across the path. A squirrel twitched his tail on a tree limb. Ants hurried about their work.

At the foot of a tall pine Dell found an ant hill. What fun it was to watch the busy workers! Farther on the path she saw some ants pushing a big, dead bug. How well they worked together! They still had a long way to go to their ant-hill home. Maybe she could help them. She watched while the ants pushed the bug on a big oak leaf in their path. Quickly she picked up the oak leaf with the ants and bug.

"Now I'll give you a ride in an airplane," she said.

She carried them carefully back to the ant hill. There she put the leaf down at their door. The ants on guard at the door were so excited. They ran about sticking their heads together, talking excitedly. But Dell couldn't understand them. Soon an army of ants got behind the bug. They pushed it off the leaf and into their ant hill.

As Dell went on the sun seemed brighter than ever. The birds sang more sweetly. The lily pool had never seemed so blue, nor the blossoms so white. The water was so clear she could see all the way to the bottom.

Soon she noticed something flapping in the grass nearby. It was a little fish that must have leaped out of the water. Or maybe some heartless boy dropped him there, Dell thought.

Quickly she picked it up and dropped him into the pool. For a minute it stayed in the same spot, its gills flapping. Then it swam behind a rock.

While Dell waited for him to come out a sunbeam darted to the bottom of the pool. It touched a pretty, rose-colored stone. Suddenly the stone flashed with rainbow colors, like a prism.

She reached into the water for the stone. But without the sunbeam it became just a rose-colored stone. The water had polished it smooth. Then a sunbeam touched it again and it flashed with many colors.

It was so clear Dell held it up to look through it. Then something magic happened. Seen through the rosy stone, the pool sparkled into fairyland. Two bugs were floating along, singing a gay song. Brown Beetle danced

4

a jig on a big lily leaf. Some tiny bugs were dancing around a lily stem like Maypole dancers. She could hear their music, too, as they kept time.

She began to hear strange new music all around her. The purple iris hummed softly as its roots drank from the pool. Lily leaves were big green bridges. Bright bugs walked on them from one shore to the other.

Dell was so enchanted she forgot about time. Too soon the sun went down. Insects hurried off to bed. Dell must go home, too. She stood up and put the magic stone in her pocket. She felt as though she had just returned from fairyland. Tomorrow she would bring her play-mates to the woods and let them look through the magic stone, too.

As she ran up the hill a rosebush caught her sleeve. When she pulled free other thorns held her. Was the Cherokee rose trying to keep her in the woods? She held up her rose-colored stone and looked through it.

Suddenly she heard a merry laugh. She turned to see a beautiful creature sitting on a Cherokee rose. Her dress was like the green moss on the lily pool rocks. Her shoes, too, were green and came to a point at the toes. On her head was a flower-shaped hat made of rose petals. Her cheeks were pink as the inside of a sea shell. The little fairy's eyes were shining as she looked at Dell. They were green, too.

"You must not take the magic stone out of the woods," she said. "I asked Cherokee Rose to hold you while I came here from the pool."

"You saw me there?" Dell asked.

The pretty creature smiled and nodded.

"But I didn't see you," said Dell.

"I hid under the rocks. I didn't want to scare you."

"I'm not scared," said Dell. "I've seen brownies a few times, but I've never seen a fairy before."

"I'm not really a fairy, my dear. I'm an undine and my work is in the water, but I often come on land to help."

"Did you come to help me?" asked Dell.

"In a way," said the undine. "I had to keep you from taking the magic stone out of the woods."

"Is it really a magic stone?" asked Dell.

"Humans may call it magic. But it doesn't seem magic to fairy folk."

All this time Dell had been looking *through* the magic stone. Now she looked *at* it. At once the beautiful music sounds died away. There was only wind in the pine tops. And what had become of the undine? She seemed to have gone from the rose blossom. Quickly Dell looked *through* the stone again. Ah, there was the undine as pretty as ever!

"I guess it is a magic stone to you," the undine said.

6

"How glad I am I found it!" said Dell.

"No one ever finds a magic stone unless she earns it."

"How? How did I earn it?" asked Dell. "I was cross this afternoon because I couldn't find my playmates. I made a little bird fall from the tree."

"But you were sorry and put it back in the tree, instead of keeping it to play with," said the undine. "And you helped some ants with their burden. And saved a little fish's life. Only those who love the little creatures can find magic stones."

"May I keep it forever and ever?" asked Dell.

"As long as you are kind to every living thing. But you must leave the stone in the woods."

Undine floated to the ground and over to an old vine-covered stump. "You must hide it here under this loose bark. Tomorrow when you come back there will be a nice surprise waiting for you."

When Dell put the stone under the bark she could no longer see the undine. But she had never been so happy as she ran back to her own garden gate. She could hardly wait for tomorrow to find out what her surprise would be.

Chapter 2

Rose-Colored Glasses

Next morning Dell was wide awake at sunrise. Her heart beat with joy when she remembered the rose-colored stone. What was the surprise the undine had promised? She dressed in a hurry. It was Saturday, so she could play in the woods all day.

As soon as she ate her breakfast off she went through the garden gate. Every blade of grass was damp with dew. The drops sparkled like Christmas tree lights. The partridge family was eating breakfast in the grain field. The mocking bird flew to her nest above the grapevine swing. She carried a berry for her babies.

Dell skipped toward the plum tree. Something shining in the sunlight made her stop suddenly. It was a pretty round spiderweb. It sparkled with dew. In the center of the web was a great big spider.

"It's a good thing I didn't run into your house, Mrs. Spider. It sparkles like diamonds."

Mrs. Spider had had a busy night catching bugs and was now sound asleep. So Dell hurried on to the old tree stump. She was eager to see if the magic stone was still there. Suddenly a droning sound made her stop. Then she saw a poor honey bee with his wing caught on a thorn. He was trying to say, "Help! Help!"

Dell did not know what to do. She had been stung by a bee once. She did not want to feel that pain again. Every time the bee tried to get away his wing tore more. Would he sting her if she tried to push him off?

Finally she decided to use a stick. She found a long twig and gently pushed the bee off the thorn. With a loud buzz that seemed to say, "Thank you!" the bee dropped to the ground. He quickly crawled under some bushes and out of sight.

With a skip and a hop Dell ran on toward the old stump. Would the undine be there? Then she saw the red mother bird she had helped yesterday. She was flying round and round the old stump. She stopped on a limb overhead and said, "Tweet! Tweet!"

She was about to swoop down on the stump when Dell saw a big green caterpillar there.

"You greedy bird!" she called. "Don't eat that caterpillar. Go get some berries."

Dell found a big leaf and helped the caterpillar crawl on it. "I'll hide you where the birds can't eat you," she said. "Then some day you can spin a cocoon and be a pretty butterfly next spring."

She hid the caterpillar under some bushes, and went back to the old stump. She knew she couldn't find her new friend, the undine, without looking through the magic stone. She looked under the loose bark and there was a most wonderful surprise. Instead of the stone she found a pair of rose-colored glasses. She laughed aloud for joy. When she put them on they fitted fine.

When she looked *through* the glasses the woods became fairyland. Birds made a chorus. Crickets played on their fiddles. Beetles beat time. Gnats, dragonflies and bees made humming sounds with their wings.

A sweet voice behind Dell said, "I hope the rose-colored glasses fit!" And there on the stump was her new friend, the undine. Suddenly Dell was no taller than the undine.

"They're simply super!" exclaimed Dell. "Thank you so much. Everything is so beautiful when I look through them. But who made them?"

"All your little friends in the woods helped."

"Please thank them for me. It is so much nicer looking through the glasses than looking through the stone. How did they make them in such a hurry?"

"I had lots of helpers. My friends, the crickets, sawed the stone in half. Some bee friends polished the glasses smoothly. You know what nice wax honeycomb they make."

"But where did you get the gold for the frames?"

"The ants brought up the gold from deep in the earth. They were thankful to you for helping them take a big bug to their nest yesterday. So they wanted to help."

"But how could ants make gold rims for glasses?"

"Mrs. Spider did that. She's the best spinner we have. She spun the gold into shape for the rims," said the undine.

"How glad I am I didn't run into her web just now!" said Dell.

"After Mrs. Spider spun the gold into long wires Mr. Beetle helped her hammer it into shape for the frames."

"But how did they make the glasses stay in the frames? Sometimes Granddad's fall out."

"Wasps helped with that. You know they make fine glue to hold their wasp nests together. They glued the glasses into the rims."

"How kind of them to do all this for me," said Dell. "I didn't know the little creatures were so smart."

"Whatever they do they do very well," said the undine. "No human beings can make honey like Honey Bee. The finest silk mills can't spin thread as fine as Mrs. Spider. Ants know better how to run their colony than people do. Everybody works together to help."

"And you help everyone, too," said Dell smiling.

"I have my special work," she said. "One of my jobs is to bathe the plants with dew during the night. I have many to help me. Everyone in Fairyland calls me Deeny Dew, because I scatter dew."

"Deeny Dew!" said Dell. "What a pretty name! What else do you do?"

"Undines have many things to do in the water. We help the water plants grow. But it is all play. We sing as water ripples over the rocks. We dance in waterfalls. We are very happy."

"Now that I have these rose-colored glasses I want to see everything in the woods. I'm not afraid of bees any more. I sure would like to know how they make honey."

"This would be a good time to visit a hive," said Deeny Dew. "It's their busy season."

Dell turned to see a big honey bee crawling on the old stump. "The woods are full of pollen and honey," Honey Bee said.

Dell was surprised she could understand everything the bee said to Deeny Dew. Then she saw it was the same bee she had helped earlier. There was still a hole in its wing.

"I would take you to my hive now," said Honey Bee, "but I had an accident this morning and can't fly very well. Please get some glue from the sweetgum tree and mend my wing."

Deeny Dew floated away to get the sweetgum. While she was gone Honey Bee said to Dell, "Thanks for saving my life. I thanked you then, but you didn't

14

know what I said."

"These rose-colored glasses help me see and hear everything now," said Dell. "I would have helped you sooner, but I was afraid of your sting. But I'm not scared any more."

"We never sting those who are kind and gentle with us. We only use our stinger when people try to kill us or steal our honey."

When Deeny Dew came back with the sweetgum she patched Honey Bee's wing. "Tomorrow your wing will be as good as new," Deeny Dew promised the bee.

"Thank you so much," droned Honey Bee. "If my wing is strong enough to fly I'll take you and Dell to see our home tomorrow."

Chapter 3

The Wax Castle

The next day Dell went to the woods as soon as she came from Sunday School. She put on her magic glasses and saw Honey Bee waiting on the stump.

"Is your wing all right today, Honey Bee?" she asked, when she was almost as small as the bee.

"I'm all whole again," droned Honey Bee.

Dell examined the wing. It had healed nicely. She swung back and forth on a limb while the bee gathered pollen. There was soft music all about. Sweet scents filled the air.

"It's so nice to have these glasses," said Dell, "so I can understand all the little creatures in the woods."

"You earned them," droned the bee. He went from one bud to the other while he talked. "I would be dead if you hadn't saved me."

"But it was Deeny Dew, who mended your wing," said Dell. "Have you seen her today?"

"She had finished painting all the plants with dew when I woke up. She will come soon to go with us."

Dell watched Honey Bee crawl into a cherry blossom. "What are you doing now, Honey Bee?" she asked.

"I'm gathering pollen. Every worker has to take a load home to feed the Queen and her babies."

"But your wing was hurt yesterday," said Dell. "When I'm sick at home I don't have to dry dishes or anything."

"Everyone must do his job in a bee hive," said Honey Bee.

"Does your Queen have to work?"

"Indeed she does! She's about the busiest one in the hive. During her life she lays about a million eggs."

Dell laughed softly. Could that be true, she wondered?

Honey Bee buzzed angrily, as if the little girl had said that aloud.

"It's the truth!" stated the bee. "She lives longer

than the workers, the drones or anyone. Workers carry her food so she can lay more and more eggs."

"I learned in school about bees," said Dell. "Drones don't work."

"So we often throw them out of the hive." Honey Bee stopped to roll some pollen into a ball and stuff it into his back leg pocket. Then he looked at Dell and said, "If I had gone back to the hive with a broken wing some worker bees would have hauled me off to die."

"How cruel!" exclaimed Dell. "Don't you have any bee hospitals?"

"Hospitals indeed! We are too busy to bother with sickness."

"You must be very hard-hearted bees," said Dell.

"Indeed we are not!" buzzed Honey Bee.

He looked so cross Dell was afraid he might sting her. Quickly she jumped from the cherry tree.

"Don't be afraid. I won't sting you," said Honey Bee. "Did you know that we die after we sting people?"

"How awful!" exclaimed Dell. "Then why do you sting?"

"To protect our hive. Every bee knows that the Queen and her babies are more important than his life."

"But why *do* bees die after they sting?" asked Dell.

"See, the stinger is under the back part of my stomach. It has a barbed end like a fish hook. When it sinks

19

into people it won't come out. A bee has to tear himself away from the stinger. This pulls away part of the stomach and makes the bee die."

"Oh, I'm sorry," said Dell. "Please don't ever sting anyone, Honey Bee. You are so nice and friendly."

Then Honey Bee went back to gathering pollen. Again Dell climbed the cherry tree to watch.

"What are you going to do with all that pollen?" she asked.

"I'll eat some of it. The rest goes in the storehouse to feed the Queen and the baby bees."

"There's lots of pollen in those rose blossoms," said Dell. She pointed to the nearby Cherokee rose vine.

"I'm getting cherry pollen. We gather only one kind of pollen at a time," said Honey Bee.

"Why?" asked Dell.

Honey Bee stopped and looked at her in surprise. "What a strange world it would be if we mixed rose and cherry pollen!"

"Honey Bee is right," said a sweet voice behind Dell.

She turned to see Deeny Dew swinging on a tree limb. How pretty she looked in her moss green dress sparkling with dew! Her cheeks were pink as the cherry blossoms. Her eyes danced like sunbeams.

"I'm so glad to see you, Deeny Dew," said Dell. "Honey Bee has been telling me so much about bees."

"She already knew some things," said Honey Bee, in his droning voice. "But she doesn't understand why I don't gather cherry and rose pollen on the same trip."

"That's why I gave her the rose-colored glasses, so she can learn about those things," said Deeny Dew. "Without the help of the bees many plants could not live. Bees carry cherry pollen from one cherry blossom to another. If he went back and forth from the rose blossoms to the cherry blossoms the pollen would be all mixed up. Then seed could not form to grow new cherry trees."

"But I thought he was gathering pollen to take home," said Dell.

"He doesn't take all of it. See how his body is covered with pollen. When he crawls into the next blossom some of the pollen will be left there."

Just then Honey Bee crawled out on a leaf. He was loaded down with honey and pollen. "I'm ready to take you home," he said.

Dell began to feel uneasy. "But how will I go there?" she asked.

"This way," said Deeny Dew. She caught Dell's hand and they floated after Honey Bee. What fun it was to sail in and out of the trees in the orchard. On the other side were the bee hives.

"The farmer keeps the bees here to help make his

cherries grow well," said Deeny Dew.

They flew among many bees returning with loads of pollen and nectar.

"Will they sting me?" asked Dell with her old fear of bees.

"No indeed!" said Deeny Dew. "Just hold my hand and everything will be O.K."

A big swarm of bees buzzed about the door of Honey Bee's hive.

"They are fanning with their wings to keep the hive cool," explained Deeny Dew. Then she laughed softly and added, "They knew about air-conditioning long before humans did."

At the door Honey Bee stopped to let the visitors

float down. Then he said, "I must store away my load of pollen first. Then I will show you around."

They followed him down a long wax hall. On each side were many small cells, like rooms in a castle. Honey Bee stored the balls of pollen in one of these. He looked smaller when he emptied his leg baskets. Then he took the visitors to a part of the hive that was not finished. Worker bees were making new cells. They watched a builder put a scale of wax in place. He mixed it with a white liquid, then smoothed it into the floor of a cell.

Next Honey Bee took them to see the Queen. She was too busy eating to notice them. The workers were feeding her royal jelly. She was much larger than the other bees. Honey Bee explained that she had no pollen pockets in her legs, nor could she make wax plates for the cells.

"She spends all her time eating and laying eggs," said Honey Bee.

"What are those workers carrying from her cell?" asked Dell.

"Those are the eggs she has laid."

They followed the workers to the cell where the eggs hatched. "In three days these will turn into grubs," said Honey Bee. "Then workers will feed them and soon they will turn into worker bees. In the next biggest cell drones will come out. And the biggest wax cells are where the queen bees are raised."

"But I thought there was only one Queen in a hive," said Dell.

"Sometimes the Queens get in fights until there is only one left," Deeny Dew whispered to Dell.

"If there are two left," added Honey Bee, "one will leave the hive. Many workers and drones go with her to make a new bee hive."

"So the plants and fruits have more and more bee helpers," said Deeny Dew. "We all work together to make the world a beautiful place."

"I must go back outside now," said Honey Bee. "We need more pollen and honey to make bee bread for the young worker bees."

When they were outside Dell said, "Thank you so much, Honey Bee, for showing me your castle. It's a wonderful place."

"And please tell your little friends to leave bees alone to do their work," said Honey Bee. "But if you are kind and gentle with us we will not sting."

Then Deeny Dew caught Dell's hand and away they floated to the woods behind her house. Dell knew it was time to go home.

"Come back again tomorrow and I'll show you more wonders," promised Deeny Dew before Dell hid the magic glasses in the tree stump.

Chapter 4

Patterns

Dell went to bed early that night. Suddenly she seemed to be floating out the window and over the garden. The moon made it bright as day. Slowly she slipped down a moonbeam into the meadow. She could hear children singing. They were dancing in a ring. Dell went closer to see what they were doing. There in the middle of the ring was a big black frog sitting on his toadstool.

 Then she noticed Deeny Dew and said, "Hi!"

Deeny glanced up from a grass blade she was painting. But there was a frown on her face.

"What's wrong?" asked Dell.

"Plenty!" grumbled Deeny Dew. "How can I cover the meadow with dew before sunrise while those children dance about?"

"You mustn't be cross with them," said a sweet voice behind Dell.

She turned to see a most beautiful creature. She wore a dress of spiderweb silk. Moonbeams floated through it, so it sparkled like diamonds. Dell had never seen her before.

"I can't help being cross, Aeriel," said Deeny Dew. "I must finish my work before the sun is up."

"The children are trying to help," Aeriel said. "They are keeping Mr. Bullfrog quiet. Last night he croaked so much people couldn't sleep."

"May I help them, too?" asked Dell.

"Their work is about done now," said Aeriel. "Mr. Bullfrog is asleep. I'll take the children out of the meadow, so you can finish your work, Deeny Dew."

"May I go with you?" asked Dell.

Aeriel smiled and took Dell's hand. "Of course," she

said. "We will go to see some new patterns."

"Dress patterns?" asked Dell.

The ring had broken up. Ned, a school friend, heard Dell's question. "Haven't you heard about the patterns?" he asked.

"Come on, we'll show Dell the patterns," said Susan, another school friend.

Dell wondered why she had been left out of this great secret. She felt better when Aeriel squeezed her hand and they floated across the meadow.

On the other side was a big cloud chariot. Aeriel tucked Dell into a downy seat. The other children piled in. Aeriel waved her wand and East Wind lifted the chariot high in the air. When Dell looked down Deeny Dew and her helpers were like fireflies in the meadow.

"Where are we going?" she asked.

"To the Sylph's palace," said a boy Dell had not noticed before.

She turned around and cried, "Why Wimpy, how did you get here on your crutches?"

How she had missed him since he broke his leg in the car accident!

Wimpy laughed gayly. "I don't need crutches in my night body," he said. "Aeriel says I'll soon be well in my day body too."

Then for the first time Dell understood what had

happened to her. She had left her heavy day body on the bed at home. In this airy, light body she did not even need her rose-colored glasses to see the fairy folk.

"Look, we're coming to the sylph's palace now," said Wimpy.

"All towers and rainbow-colored domes!" exclaimed Dell. In her joy she jumped up and down so the cloud ship rocked.

"What are sylphs?" she whispered to Wimpy.

"They are fairies of the air."

"I know undines belong to the water, but I didn't know about sylphs," she said.

"You've seen them lots of times, but you forget when you go back to your day body," he told her. "But you've been very kind lately. Aeriel says kindness opens up a door inside you. Soon you'll remember things you do in your night body."

"I'll be glad," said Dell. "Isn't Aeriel beautiful?"

"She's a Queen Sylph. The other sylphs are like her, only smaller."

They begain to hear faint, sweet music. It was louder as the ship came down near the castle wall. The children tumbled out. Aeriel led them through a gate covered with jewels.

"This is the Music Palace," said Wimpy. "They make the music patterns here."

"I never heard of music patterns," said Dell. "I only know about dress patterns."

Dell and Wimpy stayed close together when they were all inside.

"Listen," said Wimpy. "They are making a pretty pattern now."

Little wisps of music had been floating in the air. Now they ran together in a gay tune. It was like bird songs, wind in the trees and the sound of a brook all mixed together.

"That's going to be a pretty song," said Wimpy. "See what bright colors it makes, too."

"Is that what makes the pretty colors dance around?" asked Dell.

"Of course. Music has color as well as sound. You see I'm going to be a musician. That's why Aeriel brings me here to listen to the music patterns. Somebody will hear that tune in his night body. Tomorrow it will hum in his head and he will write it down on paper."

"Is *that* what they meant by patterns?" asked Dell.

"Sure. Everything has to have a pattern up in the air castles, before it comes down to earth."

"You mean houses and pictures and everything has to have a pattern?"

"Of course," said Wimpy.

Aeriel heard them and said, "Come, I'll show you

the mind pattern they are making of your new school. They will have it built by next fall."

Quick as a wink they were looking down on the lot where the new school was to be built. There was the new school just like the plans they had published in the newspaper.

"How grand it looks!" said Dell.

"But look at the assembly hall," said Wimpy. "It's all out of shape."

"That's because the pattern is not finished. The building board can't agree on how big it will be," said Aeriel.

"I didn't know our mixed-up thoughts could make such crooked patterns," said Dell.

"Come with me," said Aeriel. "I'll show you a pattern you made."

Suddenly they were in the vegetable garden behind Dell's house. They could see the beans and onions in the moonlight. In one place there was a muddy grey cloud over the vegetables. Little red darts like lightning flashed through the cloud. Then Dell remembered how cross she was when her mother sent her to weed the vegetables yesterday. She had made that dark cloud with her ugly thoughts.

"But I didn't *say* anything." Dell tried to excuse herself. "I did what Mama told me."

"But your cross thoughts made that black cloud," said Aeriel. "It kept sunlight from the plants."

"I'll try never to be cross like that again," Dell promised.

As soon as she said that she was back at the Music Palace with Wimpy.

"Now we are going to hear the King Musician play," he whispered to her. They had just gone into a very big room. "Aeriel brings me here every night. When I am older I will write down and play some of his beautiful music."

They took a seat in a corner. Soon a tall man with a golden beard came in. He sat down at a large organ. The tops of the golden pipes were lost in the clouds, for the room had no roof.

The musician began to play. Little airy notes floated

up into the clouds. They colored the clouds with rainbow hues. Then the notes ran together and made silvery ribbons that wrapped around the children.

When the musician finished Dell whispered, "I hope somebody writes down that music pattern."

"Listen now," said Wimpy, when the musician began to play again. "That's music that was written down long ago."

Then softly through the room came a familiar air. It was a waltz the musician Brahms had written down. Dell even knew words to that music. Her mother often sang it. She was about to open her mouth to sing too, but suddenly she found herself lying in bed. Out in the kitchen her mother was singing the Brahms lullaby as she cooked breakfast. Dell was back in her day body.

Chapter 5

Wings

Two days after her visit to the Music Palace Dell walked slowly to the woods. She was very unhappy. She sat down on the old stump, but forgot to put on her rose-colored glasses.

Even the song of the mocking bird did not make her feel better. She didn't even notice the squirrel who cocked his head and looked at her. He twitched his bushy tail and ran up the tree. Dell could not think of anything but dear Aunt Ellen, who had died.

How she missed her! She always had cookies or candy when Dell went for a visit. She could tell better stories than anyone. Even after she was so sick in bed she always smiled when she saw Dell.

Tears ran down Dell's cheeks. They spilled on a wild violet at her feet. Suddenly she felt something prick her ankle. She couldn't see what it was for the tears in her eyes. Again she felt the prick. Was it Deeny Dew playing tricks?

Then Dell thought of her glasses. She found them under the bark and put them on. And there was Deeny Dew! Her pert little face wore a frown.

"Stop spilling salty tears on my violets," she said.

She brushed Dell's tears away with a tiny handkerchief.

"I'm sorry, Deeny Dew," she said. "But I can't help crying. My dear Aunt Ellen died."

"Is that why you haven't been in the woods for two days?" asked Deeny.

Dell nodded and said, "She was so good to me. She gave me cookies and candy, and told the best stories in the world."

Deeny Dew sat down on the grapevine swing. She

did not look sad at all. This made Dell feel cross.

"Then you aren't sorry for your aunt. You're sorry for yourself," said Deeny Dew.

Tears filled Dell's eyes again. She was about to get real mad with Deeny Dew. But just then she thought of the gift of the rose-colored glasses. A big lump came in her throat, so she couldn't say anything.

"Yes, that's just what's the matter with you," said Deeny Dew. "You are sad because she can't give you more cookies and candy. You are not really sorry for your aunt."

"I am too!" exclaimed Dell. "It's awful to be put in a box and buried in a hole in the ground!"

"Why bless you, Dell, that wasn't Aunt Ellen in the box. It was only the body she had to wear here on earth."

"But she's gone and I can't see her here on earth!"

"But you can see her in your night body. She's living all the time now in her beautiful night body. Remember how happy you were in your night body when you went with Aeriel and Wimpy? He wasn't even crippled, you know."

"It was wonderful," said Dell. A smile helped dry her tears.

"That's how wonderful it is for Aunt Ellen now," said Deeny Dew. "She's free of that sick body she had to use down here. You saw how happy Wimpy was without his crutches."

"Only Wimpy and I had to come back to our day bodies," said Dell a little sadly.

"Then let's be happy that Aunt Ellen is free of pain."

"But I'm still sorry I won't see her anymore in her day body," added Dell.

"Oh, you will some time. You will both come back to day bodies and know each other some day. We always find those we love again."

"I'm glad you told me all this, Deeny Dew. Now I feel much better."

"Then let's forget sadness." Deeny Dew floated to the ground and caught Dell's hand. "Come. I want to show you something."

They floated down the hill. They saw a whole troop of brownies pushing some rocks about. They sang while they worked.

Dell had seen brownies a few times, even before she had her magic glasses. And once Wimpy had been with her when they saw two of the funny little fellows.

"What are they doing?" Dell whispered to Deeny Dew.

"They are moving the rocks away so that young dogwood tree can grow better," said Deeny.

Dell looked at the wet ground where a rock had been

moved. She grunted, "Ugh! Look at those ugly earth-worms!"

"Why they have been working hard to keep the ground soft in spite of the rocks," said Deeny Dew. "*I* don't think they are ugly. They are nature's helpers."

"What do they do?" asked Dell.

"They chew up the soil, so it becomes soft enough for little roots to feed on it."

"I didn't know that," said Dell.

"There would not be many trees, or other plants without the help of the earthworms, " said Deeny Dew.

"Do they work all the time?" asked Dell.

"In cold weather they go deep in the earth and rest while the trees and flowers rest. But in spring they will help the flowers and trees put on new leaves. That's the way Aunt Ellen will do also. After she rests a while in the happy land she will put on a fresh, new day body."

"Then I won't be sad any more," said Dell.

"Come on and I'll show you something else that is ready to wear a new body," said Deeny Dew.

Together they floated away through the woods. They stopped on the trunk of a big oak tree. There they saw a big brown cocoon stuck on the limb. Now that Dell was as small as Deeny Dew the cocoon looked very big. While they watched, one end of it popped open. A moist head stuck out.

"Watch! He's going to be a beauty!" said Deeny Dew. "I saw the big green caterpillar spin his cocoon before he went to sleep in it."

"Was he as big as the green one I saved from the bird?" asked Dell.

"Even bigger," said Deeny. "I helped him find many juicy leaves to eat."

"Look! He's half way out," said Dell. "But he's so wet. Will he ever get dry enough to fly?"

"Oh, yes. South Wind will blow on his wings and the sun will help."

The limp thing was now all the way out. Deeny Dew moved some leaves so sunshine would help dry him.

"He's not very pretty," said Dell.

"Just wait! See, he's beginning to push his wings out a little," said Deeny.

They watched while the sun and the breeze dried the baby butterfly. The wings seemed to grow like magic.

"Oh, see – he's going to be yellow!" said Dell, clapping her hands.

"With black spots," said Deeny.

"Look! He's spreading his wings wide. How pretty he is!" cried Dell.

The butterfly kept trying his wings. Then he took a short flight along the limb.

"It's hard to believe an ugly green caterpillar would

make such a pretty butterfly," said Dell.

"Maybe that's what your Aunt Ellen is thinking now, Dell," said Deeny Dew. "Last week she was in a tired body, full of pain. Now she's in a light, happy one, so she can move about freely."

"And when she takes a new day body I'm sure it will be as pretty as the butterflies," said Dell.

Just then the butterfly flew down to drink honey from a buttercup.

"He's on his happy way now," said Deeny Dew.

"And I must go home, too," said Dell. "I can't wait to tell Mama why we mustn't be sad any more about Aunt Ellen."

Chapter 6

The Tree Gnome

A week after they visited the Music Palace Wimpy went to school without his crutches. Dell was so glad they could now play together in the woods. They were in different classes, but they walked home together.

"Why do you look so cross?" Dell asked.

"We made soldier hats in our class, but mine was not very good," said Wimpy.

Then Dell saw the red, white, and blue hat between his books. She pulled it out and stuck it on her head.

"I think it's cute." She giggled when she looked at herself in a store window they were passing.

"Some of the others made better hats," Wimpy told her. "Teacher let the one with the best hat lead the march."

Dell knew he had wanted to lead the march, now that he was off his crutches.

"I still think it's a real cute hat," said Dell.

"You can have it," Wimpy said.

Each went on home to eat a snack. Then they met at the garden gate.

"It's been so long since we went to the woods together," said Dell.

"Let's go look for the tree gnome," Wimpy said.

They had made friends with the tree gnome long before Dell had her rose-colored glasses. As he had no magic glasses she did not wear hers either. It would be no fun unless Wimpy could see and hear the little creatures, too. How she wished he also had some rose-colored glasses!

They talked about when they first saw the tree gnome. They had started home late in the afternoon.

Suddenly there was the roly-poly gnome. He was going into his hollow tree home with a tiny lighted candle. Since then they had seen him several times.

Now they ran along the river path toward the tulip poplar tree. They sat down on the grass to wait and watch. They had learned to sit very still when watching birds. Would the gnome come out of his hollow-tree home so they could see him?

Beams of the setting sun crept into the tree hollow. Slowly they saw a puff of cloud there. It gradually turned into the tree gnome. His funny brown cap had a long tassel. He had big ears pointed at the top and a red beard pointed at the bottom. His tummy was round as a big hickory nut. But his short legs were very skinny. His brown shoes were pointed and curled up at the toes.

He was a very curious gnome. He liked to find out about people. Once Dell and Wimpy were playing in the sand with buckets and shovels. The gnome watched them. Then he ran away and soon came back with a little bucket and shovel of his own. No doubt he wanted a candle in his home after he saw lights in people's houses.

Now he ran out of his tree and raced over the blades of grass as if they were bed springs. He went skippety-hop in a circle and stopped beside Dell. Her three-cornered hat seemed to charm him. He skipped round and round her, still looking at the hat. His eyes sparkled, his pointed beard moved up and down as he talked to himself. Dell kept very still while Wimpy watched.

Quickly the gnome darted into the tree. Had they scared him? They didn't speak or move while they waited. At last there he was stepping out like a soldier. Dell and Wimpy could hardly keep from laughing. He was the proudest gnome you ever saw, wearing a three-cornered hat just like Dell's. Proudly he strutted before them. They could not keep from laughing in delight.

The laughter made the gnome stop mid-way in a strut. He stared at them curiously. Then slowly his funny face crinkled into a grin. He put his hands on his fat tummy and bent over in gales of laughter. This made Dell and Wimpy laugh even harder.

Wimpy stopped to catch his breath and said, "Let's sing the marching song and see if he will march, too."

They jumped up. Wimpy picked up a stick. He put it over his shoulder like a flag. Together they sang, "We'll march away this happy day to deeds of love and valor."

To their delight the tree gnome fell in behind them. He turned a stick in his hands as leaders do in parades. His three-cornered hat was cocked on his head like Dell's.

They marched down the river path the gayest three you ever saw. Back again they came to the hollow tree.

The sunshine was gone now. It would soon be dark. The children had to go home.

At the end of the last verse the tree gnome ran ahead. He stopped in front of his door. Suddenly his baton stick became a shining candle. He took off his three-cornered hat and bowed to his new friends. Then he backed quickly into the hollow tree and was gone.

As they hurried home Dell said, "That was the most fun we ever had."

"I'll say!" agreed Wimpy.

"Maybe the fairy folks will hear about your birthday coming soon, Wimpy," said Dell. "I hope they will plan something nice for you."

Chapter 7

Wimpy's Birthday

Dell sat in the grapevine swing. She was thinking. She had a problem. Tomorrow was Wimpy's birthday, and she had no present for him. If only he had some magic, rose-colored glasses also!

He had been so brave while his leg was hurt. He had helped her remember about the visit to the cloud castle.

He deserved something very nice for his birthday.

She jumped out of the swing and ran to the hollow stump for her magic glasses. Maybe Deeny Dew could help her. She ran down to the lily pool, but Deeny was not there. She ran up the hill to the waterfall. Undines liked to slide down as the water tumbled over the cliff.

As Dell watched the splashing water she saw a big undine leap up the falls. Her green dress changed to rainbow colors. How gay she was! She danced in the spray. At the top of the cliff she stretched her arms up. Then with a happy laugh she dived down the falling water.

Some smaller undines played at the foot of the falls. Among them Dell saw Deeny Dew. She looked prettier than ever. Her dress was like a bright soap bubble. She danced to the top of the falls with the others.

The undines stretched their arms toward the trees and flowers. Streams of light shot out from their fingers. Then they raised their arms high before they leaped back down the falls. They did this several times while Dell watched.

She was still wondering why they did it when she heard a sweet voice behind her. There was Deeny Dew standing on a rock. Her dress was splashed with water drops.

"Why did you stretch your arms out at the top of the

falls, Deeny Dew?" she asked.

"We were sending life into all the plants and blossoms."

"It must be fun!" said Dell.

"Indeed it is! We fill ourselves with energy when the spray hits us. We are almost bursting with it when we rise to the top. Then we send it out to make everything grow. That's the most fun of all—helping every living thing."

Dell smiled and said, "And I've come to ask you to help me."

"What's your problem?" asked Deeny. She seemed eager to help.

"Tomorrow is Wimpy's birthday. I don't have a present for him. I have some money in my little bank, but I don't know what to buy."

"Sometimes the best things can't be bought with money. I've never had any," said Deeny Dew. "Have you ever seen anyone happier?"

"Never," said Dell and smiled. "These glasses didn't cost money. They're the best present I ever had."

"I have an idea!" said Deeny. "Bring Wimpy to the old stump tomorrow. I'll have a present for you to give him and a big surprise."

Before Dell could say thank you, Deeny Dew was gone. A moment later she saw her playing in the waterfall again. Dell ran to Wimpy's house as fast as she could. He was so thrilled at what Dell told him, he could hardly wait for tomorrow.

Next morning early Dell heard a soft bird call. The sun was not yet up, but the eastern sky was pink. From the window she saw Wimpy waiting in the garden. She hurried into her clothes.

They crossed the meadow a few minutes later. Dell said, "I think everything looks specially pretty for your birthday."

Dew on the grass sparkled like diamonds. The birds sang birthday greetings.

"I can't wait to see what the surprise is," said Wimpy.

"We are to go to the old stump to find out," Dell told him.

She had never let Wimpy look through her glasses. Deeny Dew had told her only those who earned magic glasses could see through them. But how could she find Deeny Dew now without her glasses?

"There's nobody here," said Wimpy when they reached the stump.

He had seen brownies and gnomes, but had never seen Deeny Dew. Finally Dell said, "Turn your back and wait, Wimpy."

He turned around. Dell found her glasses and put

them on. Right away she saw Deeny Dew sitting on the stump.

"Oh, there you are!" she said in relief.

"Tell Wimpy to shut his eyes and wait for a surprise," said Deeny.

She looked toward Wimpy and said, "Shut your eyes."

Deeny felt under some loose bark and brought out another pair of magic glasses. Dell could hardly believe what she saw. They were rose-colored just like her own.

"Put them on him," said Deeny Dew.

But Dell always became small like the undine when she put on her glasses. She climbed to a bush and reached over to put the magic glasses on Wimpy.

"Open your eyes and see what you see!" she cried.

When Wimpy opened his eyes, at once he was no bigger than Dell and the undine.

"Oh! Oh!" he cried. "We're in real fairyland! Just like the beautiful things we see in our night bodies. How *did* we get here, Dell? We aren't asleep."

"It's the magic, rose-colored glasses Deeny Dew had made for your birthday. Now we can see and hear all the little creatures together."

"You earned them by being kind to every living thing, Wimpy," said Deeny Dew.

Then Wimpy saw Deeny Dew for the first time.

Dell said, "This is my undine friend, who had her helpers make our magic glasses."

"Thank you! Thank you!" said Wimpy. "Why there's music everywhere. Even the trees are humming and the brook makes music."

"Come on to the lily pool and see what's there," said Dell. They skipped down to the pool.

"Why, the water bugs are making bridges of the lily leaves," said Wimpy. "And look, I can see clear to the bottom of the pool."

"That's where I found the rose-colored stone. Deeny Dew got her helpers to make it into these magic glasses," Dell told him.

She glanced around and saw the helpers who had made her glasses.

"They made Wimpy's glasses, too," said Deeny Dew. "They've come to celebrate his birthday."

Honey Bee, with the healed wing, had brought honey from his hive. The mother bird, whose baby Dell had saved, put some wild strawberries on the lily leaf table. A squirrel brought nuts, and the ants some big cake crumbs. Deeny Dew filled buttercups with clear water. Honey Bee sweetened it with nectar. What a feast they had!

When the helpers went back to their work Wimpy and Dell ran to look for the tree gnome. They did not have to wait long before he came out of his door.

With the help of the magic glasses he looked larger to Wimpy. They were thrilled to see he still wore his three-cornered hat. He remembered their last meeting. He picked up a stick and went marching off. Dell and Wimpy kept time behind him.

"I believe he knows it's your birthday," said Dell.

As soon as she spoke the tree gnome turned around. He took off his hat and made a grand bow to Wimpy. Just as he did so the children heard the far-off sound of a breakfast bell. Quick as a wink the tree gnome ran back into his tree.

"Oh, we'll have to go home," said Wimpy.

"Wait a minute," said Dell. "We can't take our magic glasses out of the woods. Deeny Dew said we must always hide them in the old stump."

"I want to keep them on all the time," said Wimpy.

"We can't. Deeny Dew said this is our big secret. But we can come back every day and put them on and have fun," said Dell.

"It's the best present I'll get today," said Wimpy. "I thank you and Deeny Dew and all her helpers."

"I'm thrilled you earned them, Wimpy," said Dell. "It will be much more fun now that we can see all the wonderful things together."